THE POWER IN BEING KIND

HAPPINESS ACHIEVED THROUGH THE EFFECT
OF KINDNESS USING POSITIVE AFFIRMATIONS
FOR KIDS & ADULTS

RACHEL RIGGIO

D1495335

ELEVATED
PUBLISHING

TABLE OF CONTENTS

INTRODUCTION

"Kindness in words creates confidence. Kindness in thinking creates profoundness. Kindness in giving creates love."

— LAO TZU

Whoever correlated kindness and weakness was very confused. The most outstanding teachers and leaders in the world are kind; kindness, acceptance, understanding, and compassion make them great. After all, it is much easier to simply react in anger or revenge than it is to rise above hurt feelings to be kind. It is true strength to return kindness to one who has hurt you. It is true self-love to not be swayed by the insecurities of others. When you are kind, you will have no regrets. When you have no regrets, you can have full acceptance for all that is out of your control. Acceptance leads to peace.

I used to be a fighter, I fought for everything I believed in and I reacted quickly to my emotions. I always told myself that I was fighting the good fight, by bringing my direct and fierce truth to any situation without the sugar coating. Thus, I've told many people off in my life. Not only was this unhelpful, but it left them feeling negatively towards me and my perceived truths. With life's spiral of inevitable ups and downs, I became increasingly aware of my patterns and self-sabotaging tendencies. I wondered if I was acting in a way that was bringing me the outcome I desired. I started to surrender to life on life's terms, accept it and just be kind. Now that I've transcended away from the fighting, I know the paramount thing to do is return kindness when in pain and therefore live with no regrets. If I am angry with someone, bringing more pain will not initiate a healing process. My present goal is to attain peace through acceptance, compassion, and kindness. In the face of conflict, it's kindness and compassion that will change the world.

To end wars of the world, we should first practice ending wars within our communities, families, and ourselves. We are all on a mission to find peace with the ways of the world; we all have backstories that have molded us into our way of being. Like a tree that finds its way to live on a side of a mountain or through cracks in the cement, you too have adapted to your environment. Through self-awareness mixed with self-compassion, we can become the best versions of ourselves. The rewards will pervade every part of our lives.

"**Anonymously perform acts of kindness, expecting nothing in return, not even a thank-you. The universal all-creating Spirit responds to acts of kindness with the response: "How may I be kind to you?"**

— WAYNE DYER

SCIENCE OF KINDNESS

*D*id you know there is a science to kindness? Acts of kindness actually have a hormonal impact. Dacher Keltner is known as the "Kindness Scientist" from UC Berkeley. He studies the effects of being kind. Much of his research is based on Darwin's studies of 1871 that claim "Sympathy is our strongest instinct". He found that communities with higher levels of compassion would be more inclined to succeed with more offspring. Keltner found that oxytocin and serotonin were released when one did small or large acts of kindness or witnessed acts of kindness! These neurotransmitters promote wellbeing, social bonding, release endorphins and heal wounds. Being kind is good for your health! Oxytocin is also called the "love hormone" and is released when you cuddle. It does things like reduce blood pressure, makes you feel close to others, increases self-esteem, and brings optimistic thoughts. Endorphins are natural painkillers that enable you to feel better in your body. Serotonin and dopamine give you a feeling of general comfort and well-being and stimulate the reward center of your brain, offering you a sense of pleasure called the "helper's high."

There is an existing network of neurons that compassionate acts stimulate. When one acts kind and compassionately, oxytocin is released in the nervous system to promote better health. Other studies have found that compassionate humans have two times the DHEA of less compassionate people, which actually slows down the aging process! Therefore, we could say that kindness makes us more beautiful too! Cortisol is a stress hormone that can cause your blood pressure to rise among several other negative effects. It was found that compassionate people had about 23% less Cortisol in their bodies, which is significant!

Studies in neuroscience show us that if a person is in pain, it will activate the same part of the brain as a person who is witnessing someone in distress. The brain fires the same neurons in the brain when we feel pain or see someone feel pain. It also releases the same neurotransmitters for physical or emotional pain. On top of that, it releases the same neurotransmitters when experiencing pain or experiencing imagined pain (even watching a horror movie). These are significant findings because they're evidence that we're wired to feel the pain of others-- it is possible to impact our pain levels based solely on our perceptions.

KINDNESS TOWARDS OTHERS

Kindness comes from the understanding and acceptance of people. We all have our shortcomings; to give others the benefit of the doubt and be kind will cause us much less stress. Trying to change and heal other people robs them of their right to self-reliance and being controlling robs us of our own peace. When we have compassion for the suffering of others, it promotes responding with kindness. To see one's acting out as an emotional need that the person doesn't know how to express will help us come from kindness. It takes great strength and self-restraint to not react to unkind people, but to see them as suffering. To see a person whose needs are not being met, and respond with kindness, is one of the most vital traits.

Our work is in cultivating compassion. How can we have more understanding, compassion, acceptance, and gratitude in our lives? We can start by having these things for ourselves. Practicing loving-kindness inwardly will be the first step of a very personal journey to fulfillment. The meanest people in the world are living in a torture chamber in their own minds, never being able to escape the criticism. People who spend time listening to their thoughts and reconstruct hurtful messages with kindness and compassion will have started to use the power of kindness to transform their minds. Through a concept termed neuroplasticity, our brains are molded by our environments. We can re-train our minds by being aware of our thoughts. One of our greatest teachers is our social and emotional experiences. If we don't like how we feel, it means we must change our thoughts and behavior. According to Richard Davidson in his book about Neuroscience, a behavioral intervention can work better than modern medicine because it impacts specific brain circuits. When you practice kindness, inwardly and outwardly, you will feel new rushes of emotion flowing through your body.

Acts of kindness also help increase your good mood and your feeling of connection to others, thus reducing loneliness and alienation. Oxytocin is the social bonding hormone that is released through acts of compassion. When feeling depressed, it is proven that if you take your concentration off personal suffering to help another it can help lift you out of your state. Do this every day, with a mission that is tied to the wellbeing of others, and you will feel the transitions take root within you. You can cultivate that energizing feeling by practicing kindness daily. Help yourself by helping others. Humans are made to collaborate for the good of the whole. When you do this, the networks in your brain will be rearranged in a way that promotes feelings of satisfaction, fulfillment, and higher purpose. While we are taught to be self-centered, through expanding our focus to how we can be of service the way we feel will change.

KINDNESS TO SELF

his is the most important part of this book. If you cannot practice kindness inwardly, you will not be able to maintain it outwardly. All relationships stem from our relationship with ourselves. If you cannot recognize when you are being unkind to yourself, you will not recognize insensitivity or straight-up cruelty to others. Many of us are completely unaware of how we speak to ourselves.

Becoming aware of the way we talk to ourselves is the first and most important step to practicing kindness. If you have trouble finding compassion for yourself, try printing a photo of you when you were about four years old. This will help you to remember who you are, who lives inside of you, and remind you what your inner child went through. Some may need to reparent themselves by noticing an abusive parent's voice in their minds. Though we may have inner battles going on, it is through our noticing that we can begin to make positive, lasting change.

Many times there will be a physical symptom of stress that will help us realize when our negative thoughts are taking hold. You shall lovingly notice that inner critic, then take three deep breaths and repeat your affirmation with loving kindness. This will intercept the neural network--a circuit that goes in a loop firing in your brain. Through intercepting these loops with loving-kindness, deep breaths, and affirmation, we are rewiring the circuits. We have been conditioned by our life experiences to make associations from outer stimuli to emotional states. We can interrupt these "thought-to-feeling" circuits by noticing them and treating ourselves with loving-kindness.

Repeating affirmations that remind us of our true values and potential will reprogram our minds to more uplifting perspectives. Using neuroplasticity to our advantage, our minds can be molded through repetition, discipline, and sincerity. Compassion inward will pave the way for how you interact with all other life.

"Kindness is the language which the deaf can hear and the blind can see."

— MARK TWAIN

4

HOW TO USE THIS EBOOK

To get into a routine and feel the full effects of kindness in your life, pick three to five affirmations that deeply resonate with you. These should remind you of who you truly are, the big picture of why we are alive, and speak to the positive life experience that you are creating.

Repeat each affirmation ten times, for fourteen days in a row. As you will see, they are broken down into 5 affirmations per day over 14 days—all with the same promotion of the kindness/compassion theme. You can, however, pick and choose which affirmations speak to you and instead use those, and potentially repeat the same affirmations daily if that is your preference. Do not be deterred by the structure of this book, as you can make it your own.

You will notice how much easier and natural it is to do this after the first two weeks; continue until they are your unconscious habit. Listen to yourself saying them and try to focus on the feeling. Emotion is how we communicate with the universe. Emotion sends out a vibration that you invite back to you.

Writing them down can also be helpful. Put the affirmations in your car, office, on the bathroom mirror, or the refrigerator. Just keep these meaningful, life-changing sentences in all levels of your subconscious. We human beings pick up on all the subliminal messaging, which is why we find ourselves programmed to be unsatisfied, but that's another topic.

These sentences are sacred. When you say them, remember to first attempt to feel that you're already in a wholly fulfilled and abundant state. The Law of Attraction will bring these feelings back to you. Gratitude will always bring more of which to be grateful.

When your mind wanders, it's ok. Notice when this happens and with compassion for the human brain and loving-kindness towards yourself, gently return your mind to your sacred statements. Profess your affirmations to the universe to co-create your vision into the physical world.

Affirmations only take a few minutes of practice every day. Get into good habits for using them a few times per day, like when you brush your teeth, drive to work, or during meditation. As you become more aware of your thought patterns and when your inner critic starts, you can use them to interrupt these negative cycles. As you practice them, it will become easier to overcome self-defeating thoughts. As you are disciplined in your practice of stopping the cycle, you will start identifying more with the person you are becoming through these affirmations. The part of you that has been self-sabotaging with limiting beliefs will feel less and less of who you truly are. It will start to be recognized as a conditioned and learned behavior that has held you back as you lovingly release it.

If you have enjoyed this book, please help us get the message out to as many people as possible. Our intention is that we can rise in consciousness through kindness, collectively. You would really be spreading kindness by leaving a review to encourage others; the more reviews we receive the more visible this book will be! Uplifting feelings are multiplied when they are shared. Please tell us about your experiences with these techniques because we would love to know about your personal journey. Putting the life-changing technique of loving kindness out into the world will encourage others to do the same. As a result, more kindness will be invited back into your life as well.

My intention is that this book helps you to be more kind and loving to yourself and the world. I hope that through raising your awareness and consciousness that you co-create the life of your dreams with the divine. I believe in your ability to create your wildest dreams! Write it down, do guided visualizations for your dream life, make a dream board and trust the process.

DIRECTIONS

*M*ake yourself a ritual when you do your affirmations. Ideas: burn a candle, take three deep breaths, put soothing oil on your temples or sit cross-legged on the floor. Set the tone for these sacred statements respectfully and with reverence. You are inviting your desired state of being by imagining the life of your dreams while sending gratitude for its existence. You are co-creating with the divine. Emotion is how you communicate with the universe.

AFFIRMATIONS PROMOTING KINDNESS

CHOOSE
KINDNESS

Day 1

I am kind.

I am impeccable with my words.

I am full of love that others can feel when they are close.

I radiate my loving kindness inward and outward.

I am compassionate and have loving acceptance for the paths of others.

Day 2

I see the good in others.

My inner kindness shines as outer beauty.

I am Love.

I am grateful for my self-love.

I create the life of my dreams with gratitude and loving-kindness.

Day 3

I impact the world with my goodwill.

I overflow with gratitude for my life and lessons.

I am rewarded by the Universe with more opportunity and love every day.

I love to love and be loved.

I radiate compassionate thoughts, healing, and loving energy to all.

Day 4

Love and kindness are my truest nature.

I accept others with understanding, respect, and kindness.

I am compassionate and I attract compassion.

I trust the plan for my life and I rise to meet challenges with loving-kindness.

I attract abundance and all my needs are always met.

Day 5

I love myself. I trust myself. I see myself.

I attract kindness and love in my life with ease.

I am co-creating a beautiful world by coming from love in all my interactions.

I am at peace through seeing through eyes of loving-kindness and compassion.

I am doing my best alongside all my brothers and sisters in this world. I believe in the goodness of humanity.

Day 6

I appreciate my ability to come from a place of kindness in all my interactions.

I am a source of inspiration through kindness for everyone.

I joyously and gratefully share my gifts with the world. I am grateful that others share with me too.

I am grateful for my ability to share my passions, talents, and skills for the betterment of all.

My love and kindness raise my vibration and all of whom I am in contact with.

Day 7

I love myself. I am grateful for my life.

I attract healthy people and relationships in my life through kindness.

I am full of gratitude, abundance, and kindness.

I am an eternal being. My mission is compassion, love, and collaboration.

I am creating a loving, kind world with my thoughts and actions.

Completion of Day 7

*W*eek one is the hardest week of affirmations. Great work for sticking with it when it is uncomfortable. Getting in good habits is the key to reprogramming your mind for more success and abundance.

Day 8

I am filled with the love and kindness that I radiate to the world.

I radiate with kindness inwardly and outwardly.

I love unconditionally with passion, respect, kindness, tolerance, and forgiveness.

I am making the world better through kindness.

I spread positive energy and love wherever I go.

Day 9

I become stronger every day through love, compassion, and kindness.

I am grateful for all my efforts.

I am a blessing.

I am kind, loving, and confident.

I attract abundance. I spread abundant amounts of love to everyone.

Day 10

I create my future with kindness and love.

I have intention with my thoughts and words. My words and thoughts promote compassion and understanding.

Being kind is my nature.

I am deserving of abundance, success, and love.

I am worthy. I am whole. I am love.

Day 11

My kindness is the medicine for my soul.

I am free to spread my goodness in the world.

I am always taken care of by the Universe.

I am a kind, loving being that spreads love.

I love myself. My nature is full of kindness.

Day 12

I trust myself to choose kindness.

I am at one with all life. I trust the process.

I see everything through the eyes of kindness, understanding, compassion, and acceptance.

My life is my creation.

I believe in love and kindness.

Day 13

My love makes the world a brighter place.

My kindness is my nature.

I accept my pain as life lessons. I use suffering to transform my pain into strength.

I share my life with kindness, and others kindly share their lives with me.

I trust myself and my ability to respond with compassion.

Day 14

I change the world through kindness.

I value my efforts of being loving and kind in all circumstances.

I choose to be kind. I love myself for my persistence.

I am kind to myself, and I accept who I am.

Seeing the good in others makes me happier. Seeing the good in me makes me feel loved.

35 AFFIRMATIONS TO PROMOTE
KINDNESS

**FREE BONUS
MATERIAL**

TH

POWER
IN
BEING
KIND

15Ø SIMPLE ACTS OF KINDNESS

You can't just affirm kindness, you need to
practice kindness! Simple examples you can
EASILY start using towards yourself and others.

WWW.RACHELRIGGIO.COM

SUMMARY

It has been 14 days of affirmations, promoting kindness towards yourself and others. You are probably in good habits with your affirmations by now; if not, keep at it. Patience, discipline, and repetition are the foundation of reprogramming your mind. Remember, many of the things that we think are untrue, but we are addicted to and comfortable with our thought patterns.

It will take time for new thoughts to feel comfortable and natural, but you got this! You will reap the rewards of what you have sown for the rest of your life. Just like seeds, we must water them every day. Please pick your favorite 3-5 and stick with them. One day, you will notice the ease of your affirmations coming into your mind. There will be a situation in the future when you know, you would have reacted poorly in the past, but you naturally rose above old thoughts and behaviors. You will smile and feel so proud. You'll have become a better version of yourself, and you'll feel proud, confident, and loved.

Let's rise through self-love, community, and unity! And please remember to do us a kindness and <u>leave a review.</u> Please tell us about your experiences with these techniques because we would love to know about your personal journey. The more reviews we receive, the more Amazon makes our book visible. Thank you!

Customer Reviews

There are no customer reviews yet.

5 star	
4 star	
3 star	
2 star	
1 star	

Share your thoughts with other customers

Write a customer review

About the Author: Rachel Riggio

Life is such a wild ride! I never in 1 million years thought that I'd have my name on the cover of a book! Yet, writing just feels so good and comes so naturally to me! I've been on such a crazy journey from angry addiction in juvenile hall to living in peace with myself in the middle of a rice field running a school. I've been so determined to find peace in my life through all the hardships and I feel so lucky to be able to have the opportunity to write about things that have the potential to higher the vibration of our beautiful world.

Website: www.rachelriggio.com

Facebook Page: www.fb.com/Rach.Riggio

FB Group: www.fb.com/LetsRiseToThrive

Other works by the Author:

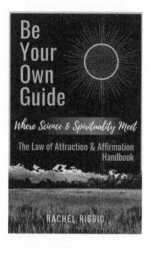

If you enjoyed this book, you will love Be Your Own Guide!

This is a guide to access your own inner guru through affirmation and self-discipline. Anyone can do it! We all have the capacity to live the lives of our dreams. Unfortunately, we were not taught these ancient techniques for success in school.

On the path where science and spirituality intersect, you can learn how to use the Law of Attraction to create your life as a best-case scenario. We were born with everything we need to thrive in this world. Each person has the ability to raise their consciousness and begin walking the self-fulfilling path to peace and abundance.

Available on Amazon.

REFERENCES

Ananda Sangha India. (2020, July 21). *Kindness | Affirmations for Self Healing*. YouTube. https://www. youtube.com/watch?v=_-Ac598nqL0

Chrissy's Point of View. (2020, December 28). *Loving Kindness Affirmations*. YouTube. https://www. youtube.com/watch?v=TEUMZgcg1g8

Garman, C. (2021). *Affirm Your Life: COMPASSION Affirmations*. Affirm Your Life. http://affirmyourlife. blogspot.com/2009/08/compassion-affirmations.html

HopeCancerResources. (2020, July 29). *Guided Affirmations for Kindness and Peace*. YouTube. https:// www.youtube.com/watch?v=eNpFo-GMRI0

J. (2021, April 22). *105 Positive Affirmations for Kids (to Build Confidence, Mindset, & More)*. Healthy Happy Impactful. https://healthyhappyimpactful.com/positive-affirmations-for-kids/

List of 94 Kindness Affirmations. (2020). B Mindful. http://bmindful.com/affirmations/kindness

Loving-Kindness Affirmations. (2020). Mindfulness Exercises. https://mindfulnessexercises.com/loving-kindness-affirmation/

Make Kindness The Norm. (2021). Random Acts of Kindness. https://www.randomactsofkindness.org/the-science-of-kindness

Meah, A. (2018a, September 26). *40 Inspirational Quotes On Kindness*. AwakenTheGreatnessWithin. https://www.awakenthegreatnesswithin.com/40-inspirational-quotes-on-kindness/

P. (2020, June 27). *42 of the Strongest & Kindness Affirmations That Work Fast*. Proper Affirmations. https://properaffirmations.com/kindness-affirmations/#Conclusion_Kindness_affirmations

Positive Affirmation Quotes (352 quotes). (2021). Good Reads. https://www.goodreads.com/quotes/tag/positive-affirmation

Ron Mick. (2017, November 12). *Loving Kindness Affirmations*. YouTube. https://www.youtube.com/watch?v=2FTEPB9R7y0

The Art of Kindness. (2020, May 29). Mayo Clinic Health System. https://www.mayoclinichealthsystem.org/hometown-health/speaking-of-health/the-art-of%20kindness#:~:text=Kindness%20has%20been%20shown%20to,be%20healthier%20and%20live%20%20longer

Thechery Kids. (2020, December 12). *Kindness Affirmations*. YouTube. https://www.youtube.com/watch?v=BDYBOwhnGGQ

Using the Practice of Self-Kindness to Cope With Stress. (2018, June 19). Psychology Today. https://www.psychologytoday.com/us/blog/the-compassion-chronicles/201806/using-the-practice-self-kindness-cope-stress

Made in the USA
Las Vegas, NV
28 April 2022